Mother Teresa:

A Life of Love

Written by John Monette
Illustrated by Marieta Monette

Liguori

To Belisario Cornejo Puertolas

Imprimi Potest:
Stephen T. Rehrauer, CSsR, Provincial
Denver Province, the Redemptorists

Published by Liguori Publications
Liguori, Missouri 63057

To order, visit Liguori.org or call 800-325-9521.

ISBN 978-0-7648-2708-2

Photo of Mother Teresa by Manfred Ferrari, December 1985; from Wiki Commons, 2003

Liguori Publications, a nonprofit corporation, is an apostolate of the Redemptorists.
To learn more about the Redemptorists, visit Redemptorists.com.

Printed in the United States of America
20 19 18 17 16 / 5 4 3 2 1
First Edition

Mother Teresa

A Life of Love

By John Monette
Illustrations by Marieta and John Monette

This is the story of a girl named Agnes.

Agnes was very brave. She left her family
and home to travel far away. She answered God's call
and became a sister. She gave up what she had
to serve poor people in India.

Today we call her Mother Teresa.

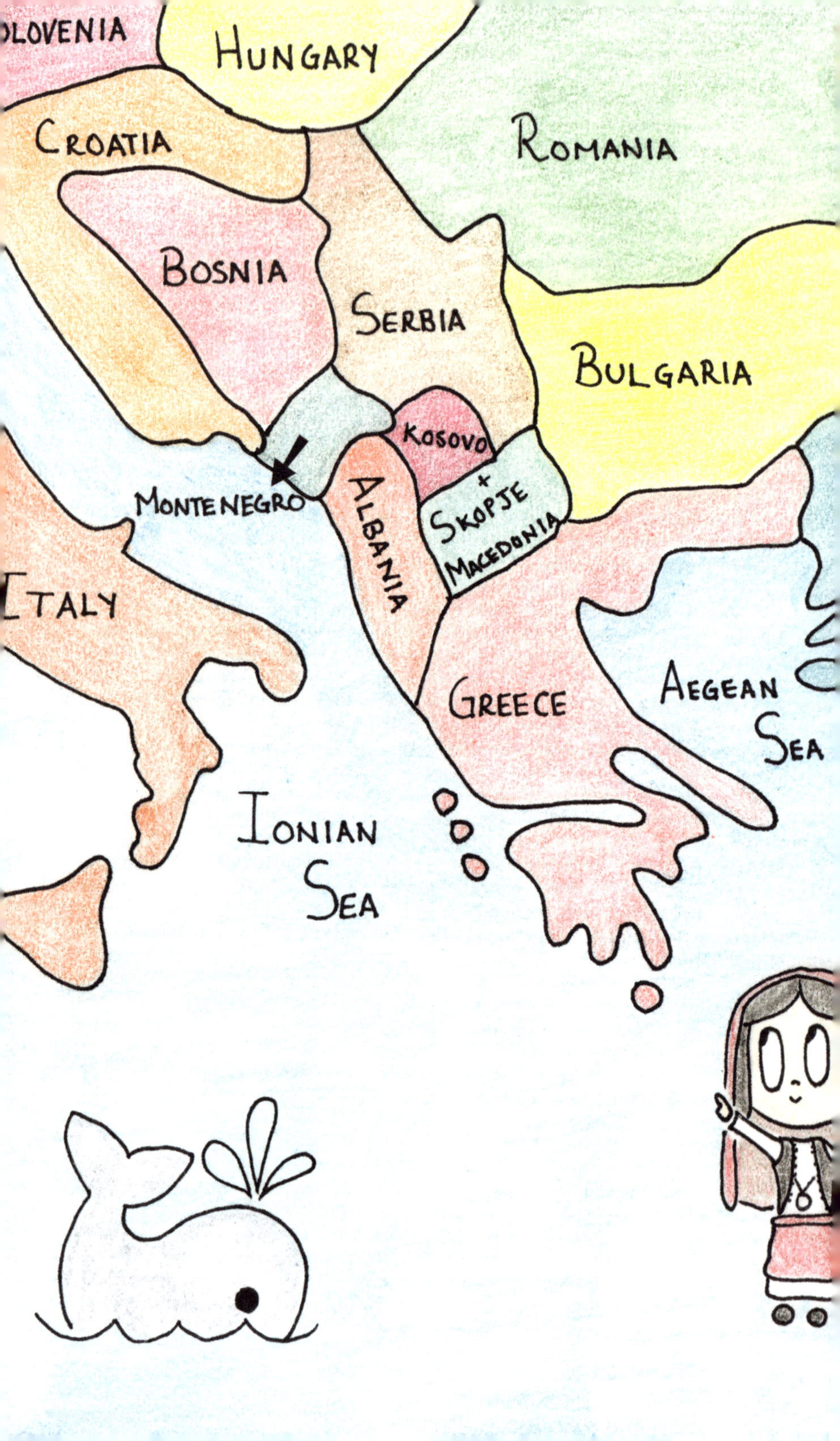

SLOVENIA
HUNGARY
CROATIA
ROMANIA
BOSNIA
SERBIA
BULGARIA
KOSOVO
MONTENEGRO
ALBANIA
SKOPJE
MACEDONIA
ITALY
GREECE
AEGEAN SEA
IONIAN SEA

Mother Teresa was born on August 26, 1910.
She was born in a little village called Skopje (SKO-PYE).
Today, Skopje is the capital of Macedonia, a country
in southeastern Europe.

Her parents named her Gonxha (Gohn-jay) Agnes.
Gonxha means "rosebud" or "little flower" in Albanian.

She was baptized the next day, on August 27.
This day was very important to Agnes and her family.
They celebrated it instead of her birthday!

Agnes was the youngest in her family.
Her older brother's name was Lazar.
Her older sister's name was Aga.

Her mom, Drane, stayed at home and took care of the family. Her dad, Nikola, worked very hard. He was a builder.

Agnes loved her family. They were very happy together, even when Agnes had to do chores when she'd rather play.

Agnes' parents really loved God.
They shared their love for God with Agnes.

Agnes knew she only had to go to Mass on Sundays, but she went every day! Jesus was her best friend, and she wanted to see him all the time.

Agnes also talked to Jesus every day in prayer.

Agnes' parents taught her to care for others, especially the poor. Her father gave them money and things they needed. Her mother visited the poor and brought food to them.

Agnes always went with her mother on these visits, and she enjoyed playing games with these neighbors.

Her faith taught her Jesus' words:

"For I was hungry and you gave me food,
I was thirsty and you gave me drink....
whatever you did for one of these
least brothers of mine, you did for me."

Agnes loved the poor just like she loved Jesus!

But when Agnes was eight,
something bad happened, a tragedy.

Her father came home from work feeling very sick.
He went to the hospital.
The doctors worked hard, but they could not help him.

Agnes' father died. She was very, very sad.

Agnes missed her father very, very much.
Her mother missed him, too.
Some days, she couldn't even get out of bed.

Without her father working to make money,
Agnes' family became poor. Her mother went to work
to help get money to take care of them.

Even though they were now poor,
Agnes and her mother still helped their neighbors.

Agnes loved helping the poor.
She read stories about priests and nuns
who helped poor people in faraway places.

Agnes met two priests from India. They had left
comfortable lives to live with the poor. They did things
Jesus would do. They cared for sick people.
They brought water to the thirsty. They fed the hungry.

Many people learned about Jesus through them.

Agnes liked their stories a lot.

When the priests left, Agnes still thought about India.

Maybe she could be a missionary, too!
A "missionary" is someone who travels far away
to talk about Jesus with people who don't know him.
Missionaries also care for the poor and teach.

Agnes really liked the idea! But she was still little.
She decided to wait until she was older.

Agnes kept growing closer to Jesus and his Mother, Mary. She said a rosary every day. She wanted to be like Mary when she grew up.

On August 15, 1928, the feast of the Assumption of Mary, Agnes went on a "pilgrimage," meaning a journey to a holy place. She went with her family and church members. They went to the Shrine of the Black Madonna in nearby Letnica.

Agnes prayed in front of the statue of the Black Madonna. She heard the voice of God! God called her to become a nun and serve him and the poor.

Agnes couldn't decide which order of sisters to join.
There were so many!
The Carmelites, Dominicans, Benedictines, Franciscans...

Where did God want her to go?

Then Agnes found the Sisters of Loreto, who lived in Ireland. But they did missionary work in India! Agnes asked if she could join, and they said, "Yes."

On September 28, 1928, Agnes said goodbye to her family and went to join the sisters.

On October 12, Agnes made it to Ireland.
As a "novice," a sister-in-training,
her job was to pray and work very hard.

DICTIONARY
DICTIONARY
ALBANIAN-
ENGLISH

Agnes was also working to be a missionary in India. She had to learn three new languages: English, Bengali, and Hindi.

It was hard work!

But in a few months, Agnes was ready.

Ireland
Europe
Asia
Africa
India
N
W
S

Today, if you wanted to travel to Calcutta (now called Kolkata) in India, you'd take a plane. There were no planes for Agnes. She had to take a boat.

The boat sailed on the Atlantic Ocean,
across the Mediterranean Sea,
through the Suez Canal,
and across the Indian Ocean.

Finally! She was in India on January 6, 1929. The trip took two months!

On May 25, 1931, Agnes made "vows," or promises to God, to live in poverty, chastity, and obedience. That meant she wouldn't ask for more than she needed. She would live for God and do what he asked.

After her vows, she changed her name to Teresa after St. Thérèse of Lisieux.
Saint Thérèse is the patron saint of missionaries.

Capital Cities
India: NEW DELHI
PERU: Lima
Spain: Madrid

Sister Teresa taught the catechism and geography at St. Mary's School for girls in Calcutta.

In 1937, she made her "final vows." That meant she was a full sister in her religious community. She would serve God for the rest of her life. She also became principal of St. Mary's. People started calling her Mother Teresa.

खान मार्किट
जूता

But Mother Teresa felt something wasn't right. There was a thought she kept having.

She was comfortable, but many in India were not. There was a man outside her window who slept in a gutter. He was dirty, sick, and hungry. No one cared about him.

There were thousands of men, women, and children like him in Calcutta.

Mother Teresa knew she would have three meals a day.
It wasn't fancy food, but it was good.

When she ate, she thought about all the people who
didn't have enough. She wanted to help.
She wanted to help right then!

Mother Teresa brought her plate outside.
She gave her meal away to someone
who needed it more.

Mother Teresa felt God was calling her
to feed the hungry.

On September 10, 1946, Mother Teresa got on a train to go to Darjeeling. She wanted to go somewhere quiet so she could hear Jesus better.

While she prayed the rosary, Jesus spoke to her:

"I thirst, and I want you to serve me in the poorest of the poor."

Mother Teresa knew what to do.
She would leave home again. She would live with the poorest of the poor and serve them.

Mother Teresa needed permission before she could start her new work. She'd have to ask some important people. It wasn't going to be easy!

First, she went to Fr. Van Exem. He was her spiritual director, helping her understand the will of God in her life. He told her she'd have to ask the Archbishop of Calcutta.

She asked Archbishop Perier.
He listened but didn't like the idea. "No!" he said.

So Mother Teresa went to her mother superior, the sister in charge of the convent where she lived, and asked her. She also said, "No!" She sent Mother Teresa to teach in a village called Assandh instead.

Mother Teresa was sad,
but she did what she was told.

And she sent a letter to Pope Pius XII.

Pope Pius XII read Mother Teresa's letter. He liked what he read, and he granted her wish! Now Mother Teresa could live and work among the poor.

Mother Teresa was excited! She knew how to beg for food and water. She knew how to teach children. She knew how to spread God's love. But she didn't know how to take care of sick people.

Before Mother Teresa could help the poorest of the poor, she would have to go to nursing school.

She went to the Medical Mission Sisters in Patna, where she learned how to clean sores, dress wounds, give shots, and deliver babies.

Now that Mother Teresa was ready to work with
the poor, she wanted to dress like them.
The women in India wore saris and sandals.
So, Mother Teresa needed a sari and sandals, too!

At the sari shop, she saw the finest, most expensive
saris. They came in beautiful colors.
They had nice designs. They were made from soft silk.

But none of those was right.

Mother Teresa chose a plain,
white sari made of cotton.
It had a blue border for our Blessed Mother Mary.

Mother Teresa started her work with the poor on August 17, 1948. She felt alone on the streets of India. She thought about going back to her comfortable life. But she wasn't really alone. Jesus was with her!

Her new home was a one-room hut.
She didn't have furniture. It didn't even have a floor!
It was hot inside. There was no air conditioning,
no running water, not even a bathroom!

But Mother Teresa didn't give up.

One day, Mother Teresa began teaching.
She only had five students. They didn't have a blackboard or chalk, so they used the dirt floor to write on.

After one week, there were twenty-five students.
More children came every day!

Mother Teresa taught all kinds of things, like math and geography.

But that wasn't all she did...

Mother Teresa visited all her neighbors. She offered to help with anything she could.

There was a lot of suffering in Calcutta, and Mother Teresa wanted to help. She met a blind man in rags, so she found him some clothes. She saw a sick woman on the side of the road, so she took her to a hospital. She saw poor children looking for food in the garbage, so she begged for food for them in the market.

MISSIONARIES
OF
CHARITY

So many people needed help. Mother Teresa couldn't do it alone. One day, some of her old students came to visit her. They wanted to help, too!

Her helpers just kept coming! Eventually, she had so many helpers they became a new order of sisters. They were called the Missionaries of Charity. They would spend their whole lives helping the poor.

Mother Teresa began to win many awards for her good works. Some of the awards were very important, like the Nobel Peace Prize.

Others came from important people. One came from the president of the United States!

But that didn't matter to Mother Teresa. She was helping the poor, because Jesus had asked her to:

"Whatever you did for one of these least brothers of mine, you did for me."

I Thirst

Even when Mother Teresa was old and sick,
she didn't stop helping the poor.

On September 5, 1997,
Mother Teresa went home to Jesus.
She was 87 years old.

On October 19, 2003,
Pope St. John Paul II beatified Mother Teresa,
making her one of the blessed.
A few years later, on September 4, 2016,
Pope Francis canonized her, declaring her a saint!

Even though she's in heaven, her mission continues.
Her Missionaries of Charity serve and care
for the poor today.

Mother Teresa, Pray for Us!

Mother Teresa,
I have a short prayer
I want to say.
I know how much you care for people in need
and how much you care for little kids like me.

Ask Jesus to help me be a good kid.
To think about other people more than me.
To care for other people more than me.
To love other people more than me.

Starting at home,
with my mom and my dad,
my sisters and brothers.

Help me to be nice to those who live around me.
Help me to follow Jesus' words,
"Whatever you did for one of these least brothers of mine,
you did for me."

Amen.

Dear Parents,

We hope that you and your children have enjoyed reading about Mother Teresa. Here are some ideas for continuing their education in our faith:

- As a young girl, Mother Teresa became a friend of Jesus by spending time with him. You can help your kids become Jesus' friend by leading them to him through going to Mass and receiving Communion.
- Mother Teresa's parents taught her the importance of looking after others, especially those most in need. Maybe you can volunteer as a family at a local soup kitchen or a nursing home. This way, you teach your kids by your own example.
- Mother Teresa's soul was well-prepared by prayer and service, so that when Jesus called her to leave her family and consecrate her life as a nun, she was ready. As parents, you can also prepare your kids to listen to Christ's calling.
- You can teach your kids that earthly rewards and personal success don't matter quite as much as what we do for one another and for God. Hopefully, like Mother Teresa, we always keep our eyes focused on our eternal reward in heaven.

God bless you and your children,

Marieta and John